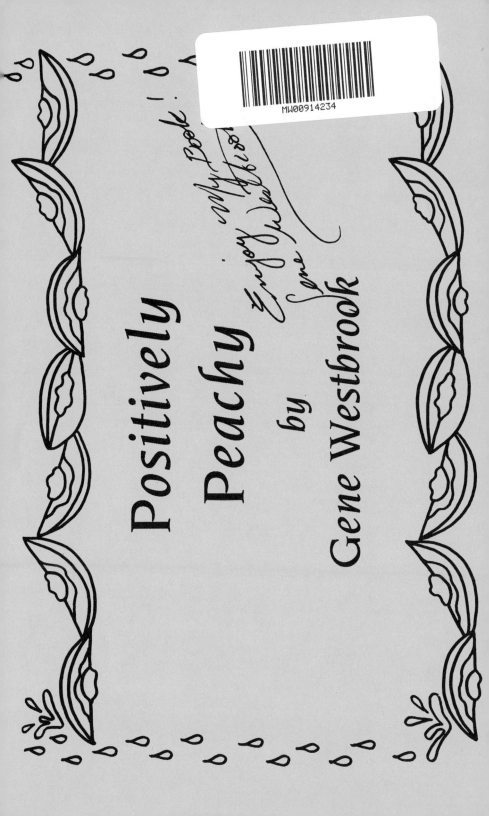

# Positively Peachy

Enjoy why book!
Gene Westbrook

by

Gene Westbrook

Copyright © 1990
by
Gene Westbrook Publications, Inc.
Millbrook (Montgomery), Alabama

*****************************************************************

To Order Additional Books:

POSITIVELY PEACHY
P.O. Box 869
Millbrook (Montgomery), Alabama 36054

*****************************************************************

OTHER COOKBOOKS BY GENE WESTBROOK: THE MAGNOLIA COLLECTION AND PIGSKIN PARTIES        By GENE WESTBROOK

Third Edition        February 1995        40,000 copies in print

Cover Design and Illustrations by GENIA WESTBROOK
Back Cover Photograph by JOE WESTBROOK
Editor Isabelle V. Hanson
Recipe Tasters JAY WESTBROOK and ALMAND WESTBROOK
Printed in the USA by EBSCO Media, Birmingham, AL

ISBN 0-9614247-2-9        Library of Congress No. 90-070947

# About the Artists and Photographer

Genia Westbrook is first and most importantly my daughter. She is a graduate in Visual Art and Design from Auburn University, Auburn, Alabama. Her first endeavor in book design was accomplished while still a student. She designed the covers and divider pages for our first cookbook, THE MAGNOLIA COLLECTION. In 1989, she designed the covers for our PIGSKIN PARTIES cookbook. And now, her visual graphic talents are used most pleasingly for the front cover of this book along with the artwork presented on the interior pages.

Joe Westbrook is both my husband and my friend. He is a corporate pilot by profession and a very talented man in many other fields including art and photography. His photography was used for illustration models in THE MAGNOLIA COLLECTION and his artistic talents used for the divider page art and recipe art in PIGSKIN PARTIES. He has provided the taste-appealing photograph for the back cover of this cookbook along with artwork for the interior pages.

## About the Recipe Tasters

Jay and Almand Westbrook are my sons and assistants in many varied areas. They usually are most enthusiastic in the area of taste-testing for a new cookbook and somehow manage to have a few assistants of their own!

# Foreword

Peaches are such a wonderfully versatile fruit. The recipes in POSITIVELY PEACHY will perhaps give you some fresh, new ways to enjoy peaches along with some classic recipes that have been used for many, many generations. You may even find a long-lost recipe.

Just buying fresh peaches is such a pleasant experience. I had stopped at a fruit stand to buy peaches for testing this cookbook. As I stepped from my car, I got a whiff of pure heaven – the delicious fragrance of PEACHES filled the air!

In my recipes, peaches can be served as appetizers, in beverages, as an ingredient in entrees, in sweet breads, and, of course, in a spectacular array of desserts. They can even be used as an aromatic center-piece for your dinner table – mound whole, unpeeled peaches in a beautiful crystal bowl and tuck-in small sprigs of fresh mint. Let your imagination wander to suit the occasion and your own tastes.

*Gene*

OTHER COOKBOOKS BY GENE WESTBROOK:

*THE MAGNOLIA COLLECTION*
*PIGSKIN PARTIES*

# Table of Contents

# Acknowledgments

## My very Special Thanks

To my husband, Joe, and our three children, Genia, Almand, and Jay. There is just no way POSITIVELY PEACHY cookbook could have been written without all of your help. From artwork to grocery shopping, cooking, taste-testing (the fun part), cleaning (the drudgery part), being sounding boards, and generally putting up with my full-steam-ahead craziness.

To my mother, who has been invaluable. She has provided the "Peachy Ideas" section on easy peeling and freezing of peaches along with grocery shopping and cooking.

To my husband's mother, Ann Harris for always being willing to help me out, for her encouragement, and for sharing Joe with me.

To all my extra special relatives that continue to encourage me to write cookbooks and generously contribute their recipes: Lucile Williams, Tommy and Linda Sparks, Scotty Sparks, Dorothy and Dan Kuerner,

Mary and James Keck, Helen and Grif Carden, Alice and Jack Roberts, Joan and Jim Backes, Diane and Mike Presley, Woody and Cecelia Pfeiffer, Bruce and Debby Pfeiffer, Elizabeth Sparks, Trey and Ellen Sparks, and Beth and Dean Fulghom.

To Alice Roberts and Brenda Whitaker for their special recipes and to Terry Martin for her expertise.

To our many friends who keep our books selling and always seem to be pleased to help whenever we ask. We can't do it without you!

Once again to Isabelle Peat for editing POSITIVELY PEACHY. You do more than just edit, you do it with love. Thanks to David and their children for loaning her.

All recipes in this book have been made, tested, and enthusiastically enjoyed by my family, friends, and relatives.

# SOME PEACHY IDEAS

As a general rule, take care to avoid any bruising of your peaches in the picking process or in the preparation process. The peaches should be both ripe yet still firm. Very soft peaches will not cook or freeze well.

## To Peel Easily:

1. Place the peaches to be peeled in a colander, very thin cloth bag, the basket, or drop directly into a deep pot of boiling water for approximately one minute. Make sure that the entire peach is submerged and that the peaches are free enough for water to flow all around them.

2. After the one minute in the boiling water, immediately plunge the peaches into cold water. You may need to add a few ice cubes to keep the water cold.

3. The skin should come off the peach in large peels.

4. If peaches are slightly under-ripe, allow them to remain in the hot water a little longer to loosen the peel. It will also improve their flavor.

## To Freeze:

1. Select varieties that are most suitable for freezing that are grown in your area. Your State Department of Agriculture can provide the information.

2. Freeze within 12 hours of picking time, if possible.

3. Prepare and freeze peaches only about 3 pints at one time. Then repeat the process until all peaches are frozen.

4. Make a syrup of three cups sugar per four cups water for a medium sweetness. Peaches should taste slightly sweeter than desired at this stage to be the proper flavor after freezing. Simply stir the sugar into the water to dissolve.

No heating is necessary.

5. Add an ascorbic acid mixture bought at the grocery store and follow the directions on the package.

6. Pack sliced peaches into polyethylene containers, allowing room to add about $^1/_2$ cup of sugar syrup, and allowing about $^1/_2$ inch per pint expansion room. More room will be needed for larger containers. Pack the containers to force out as much air as possible since air dries out the peaches when frozen.

7. Place tops on containers according to manufacturer's instructions.

8. Label and date containers.

9. Place containers as quickly as possible into the coldest part of your freezer allowing room around the containers to promote fast freezing. Containers can be packed more economically space-wise after one day of freezing.

10. Thaw in the refrigerator in the container.

*This is not the only method to use. You may have a method that you prefer that has been successful.*

## Measurements:

1. About 2 medium to large peaches = 1 cup sliced peaches.

2. About 4 medium peaches = 1 cup pureed peach.

## Substitutions:

In most recipes, frozen or canned peaches can be substituted for fresh peaches. The frozen and canned peaches have already been sweetened; therefore, the amount of sugar called for in a recipe will have to be adjusted. Also, the peaches should usually be drained before using.

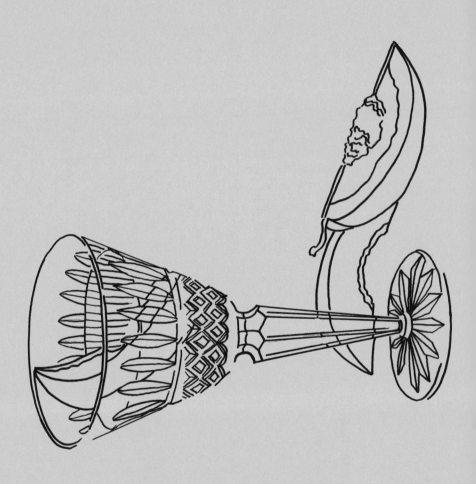

# Beverages

## Georgia Julep

| | |
|---|---|
| 1 | medium fresh peach, chilled |
| 1 | tablespoon sugar |
| 2 | ounces bourbon |
| $1/_2$ | julep cup shaved ice |
| | mint sprigs |

Wash, peel and slice the peach; then puree in a food processor or blender with sugar. Stir in the bourbon and pour over the shaved ice. Garnish with mint sprigs.

*Honey Chile, this ought to make yo' fan flutter!*

# Texas Peach Daiquiri

| | | | |
|---|---|---|---|
| 4 | large ripe peaches | 2 | ounces Rose's lime juice |
| 1/4 | cup granulated sugar | | Crushed ice |
| 4 | ounces rum | | |

Wash, peel, and cut peaches into a blender; add sugar and puree. Blend in the rum and lime juice. Add crushed ice a small amount at a time until daiquiri mix is slushy.

# Florida Fandango

| | | |
|---|---|---|
| 1 | fifth dry red wine | Lemon Slices |
| 1 | ounce Triple Sec | Lime Slices |
| 1 | cup brandy | Orange Slices |
| $^1/_2$ | cup lemon juice | 2 cups diced fresh peaches |
| $^1/_2$ | cup granulated sugar | $1^1/_2$ cups club soda |

Mix wine, Triple Sec, brandy, lemon juice, and sugar. Add lemon, lime, and orange slices. Cover and refrigerate overnight. One hour before serving, sprinkle peaches with extra brandy and add to the wine mixture. At serving time add the club soda, and stir.

# Peach Alexander

| | |
|---|---|
| 2 | large fresh peaches, chilled |
| 1/2 | cup brandy |
| 1/2 | cup creme de cacao |
| 1 | quart vanilla ice cream |

Wash, peel, and slice the peaches. Place the sliced peaches into a blender along with the remaining ingredients. Blend thoroughly. Pour into the champagne glasses to serve.

*Alexander was definitely great! This is fabulous.*

# Peaches 'n Champagne

## Beverages

4    medium peaches
1    fifth champagne, chilled

Wash fresh peaches, then peel and slice into wedges. Place 2 peach wedges into each champagne glass, then fill the glass with the chilled champagne.

*Simple and elegant!*

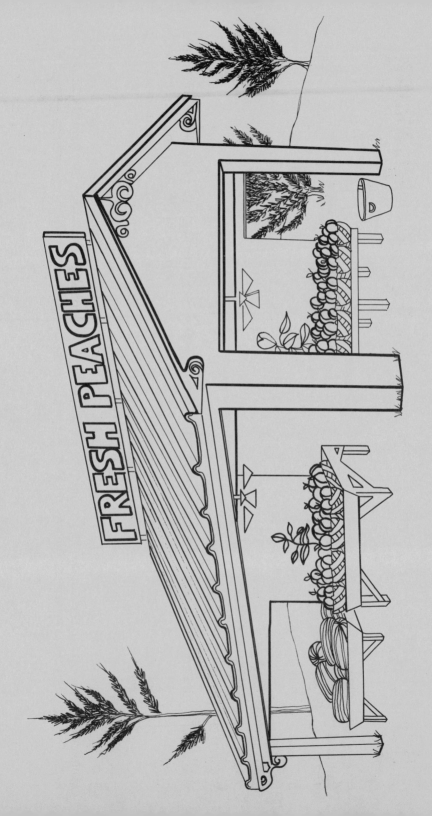

# Entrees

## Chicken Maxwell

| | |
|---|---|
| 6 | boneless, skinless chicken breast halves |
| | Salt and pepper |
| 3 | fresh peaches; washed, peeled, and diced |
| $1/2$ | cup onion, finely chopped |
| $1/2$ | cup cashews, chopped coarsely |
| $1/2$ | teaspoon ground ginger |
| $1/4$ | cup margarine, melted |
| | Toothpicks |

Sauce:

| | |
|---|---|
| 1 | (8 ounce) carton sour cream |
| $1/4$ | cup brown sugar |
| 2 | teaspoon Dijon mustard |
| 1 | tablespoon brandy |
| $1/4$ | teaspoon salt |

Place each chicken breast on waxed paper, and flatten to $1/4$-inch thickness using a meat mallet or rolling pin. Sprinkle the chicken on both sides with salt and pepper. In a bowl, combine all the remaining ingredients except the margarine. Divide the peach filling evenly placing about $1/4$ cup in the center of each breast. Fold the chicken over the filling, and secure tightly with toothpicks. Place the melted margarine in a 9" x 13" baking pan, and coat the bottom of the pan. Place the stuffed chicken breasts, top side down, in the margarine. Bake at 375° for 25 minutes; then turn chicken and bake an additional 20 minutes. Ten minutes before serving the chicken begin to make the sauce. In a saucepan over low heat, combine all the sauce ingredients, and cook on low for 8 minutes. Do not let the sauce boil. Serve the hot sauce over the chicken breasts. Serves: 6.

# Michigan Chicken Almondine

Sliced almonds
4-6   chicken breast halves, boned
1      cup peach preserves

½    onion, chopped
½    teaspoon garlic salt
½    cup barbecue sauce (catsup base)
2      tablespoons lite soy sauce

Toast the almonds until they are a light tan color, taking care not to overcook since they are very thin; set aside. Place the chicken breasts into a greased baking dish. In a small bowl, blend together the remaining ingredients, and spread over the chicken breasts. Bake, uncovered, at 350° for 45 minutes. Sprinkle with the toasted almonds just before serving. Serves: 4-6

*This tangy, not-too-sweet dish is particularly good served with the sauce over hot white rice. It's so versatile that I serve it for dinner parties, luncheons, and for dinner at home.*

# Chicken California

| | |
|---|---|
| 6 | boneless chicken breast halves, skinned |
| 3/4 | cup soy sauce (lite can be used) |
| 1/4 | cup brown sugar |
| 1 | tablespoon vegetable oil |
| 2 | tablespoons vinegar |
| 1 | large garlic clove, minced |
| 1 | medium onion, sliced |
| 3 | large fresh peaches; washed, peeled, cut in wedges |
| | Cooked white rice |

Wash chicken, and drain; then score diagonally 4 times making cuts deep, but not cutting through the chicken. Place chicken in a flat glass dish. In small bowl, combine the remaining ingredients; except the peaches and rice. Mix well to dissolve the sugar. Pour the sauce over the chicken, and turn chicken several times. Cover and refrigerate for 1 hour; turn twice. Reserve sauce after removing chicken. Cook chicken on a hot grill until it is done. While chicken is on the grill, simmer the remaining sauce until the onions are tender. Just before serving, drop the peach wedges into the hot sauce. Serve the hot sauce over hot rice topped with a chicken breast.

# South Carolina Chicken Salad

*Make the salad the day before serving and refrigerate overnight.*

| | | | |
|---|---|---|---|
| 2 | cups cooked chicken, cut in large cubes | 1/2 | cup mayonnaise |
| 3/4 | cup thin-sliced celery | 2-3 | large fresh peach halves |
| 1/4 | cup slivered almonds, toasted | 1 | large fresh peach; peeled and |
| 1 | teaspoon salt | | cut in wedges for garnish |
| 1/4 | cup sour cream | | Cream cheese |
| 1 | cup seedless green grapes, halved | | Red-tip lettuce cups |
| 2-4 | teaspoons lite soy sauce | | Paprika |

Combine all ingredients except cream cheese, lettuce, and peaches until well mixed. Cover and refrigerate overnight. Before serving, place a small dollop of cream cheese in center of lettuce cup, and seat the peach half in the cream cheese to hold in place. Repeat this process with the lettuce on the serving plate. Fill the peach halves with the chicken salad, and garnish with a peach wedge sticking in the top of the salad. Sprinkle with a little paprika for color.

*Seating the peach on the serving plate should prevent unidentified flying objects at the table. Unfortunately, that does cut out some of the fun! It reminds me of the time my whole Maine lobster took flight at a dinner party – gave everyone a great laugh.*

# Pennsylvania Peach Ham Slices

2-3    large peaches; washed, peeled,
and cut into wedges

4    tablespoons brown sugar

1/4    teaspoon dry mustard

2    tablespoons vinegar

1    tablespoon lite soy sauce

6    buffet ham slices, 1/4-inch thick
(ham should already be cooked)

In a spray-greased, 10-inch skillet, mash the peach wedges and blend all the ingredients except the ham. Cook over medium to low heat until peaches begin to soften; then add the ham slices. Simmer until the sauce thickens and cooks into the ham, about 10 minutes.

*Turkey ham slices can be substituted for the pork. The slices can also be cut into bite-sized pieces and served as an appetizer in a chafing dish.*

# Pork Tenderloin with Peach Glaze

3   fresh peaches, mashed
2   cups water, divided
¹/₂  cup granulated sugar
¹/₄  teaspoon dry mustard

1   tablespoon soy sauce
¹/₂  teaspoon salt
2   pork tenderloins (about 1 pound each)
Salt and pepper

Preheat oven to 325°. Place mashed peaches, 1 cup of the water, and sugar in a saucepan. Bring to a boil, then reduce heat and simmer for 45 minutes. Mix mustard, soy sauce, and salt into the glaze; cook an additional 5 minutes. Salt and pepper the tenderloins, then place in a greased baking pan with the remaining 1 cup of water. Bake 30 minutes per pound (total weight of both tenderloins) in a preheated oven at 325°. During last 30 minutes of baking time, pour glaze over the roast. Baste roast with the glaze several times during the last 15 minutes of cooking time. Serves: 4.

# Pork Chops with Peaches and Cashews

| | | | |
|---|---|---|---|
| 6 | loin pork chops, $3/4$-inch thick | 1 | teaspoon ground ginger |
| Salt and pepper to taste | | $1/8$ | teaspoon dry mustard |
| 3 | tablespoons vegetable oil | $1/8$ | teaspoon garlic powder |
| 1 | cup sliced fresh peaches | Water | |
| 2 | tablespoons brown sugar | $1/2$ | green pepper, slivered |
| 1 | medium onion, sliced in rings | Hot rice | |
| 2 | tablespoons soy sauce | $1/2$ | cup cashews, coarsely chopped |

Sprinkle chops with salt and pepper on both sides of meat. In a skillet, heat oil, and brown chops on both sides; then remove from skillet. Drain all except 2 tablespoons of drippings from skillet. Add peaches, sugar, onions, soy sauce, ginger, mustard, garlic powder, and about $1/4$ cup water; blend well. Return chops to skillet on medium heat, and coat with sauce. Cover skillet, and simmer for 30 minutes. Add green pepper slivers; simmer 5 minutes longer. Serve over hot rice and top with cashews. Serves: 6.

# Breads & Butter

## Peach Pecan Bread

| | |
|---|---|
| $1/2$ | cup vegetable shortening |
| 1 | cup sugar |
| 2 | eggs, slightly beaten |
| $1^1/4$ | cups plain flour |
| 1 | teaspoon baking powder |
| $1/4$ | teaspoon salt |
| $1/2$ | cup milk |

| | |
|---|---|
| $1/2$ | cup pecans, finely chopped |
| | Powdered sugar |

Glaze:

| | |
|---|---|
| 1 | large peach, mashed to produce 3 tablespoons juice (discard pulp) |
| 1 | tablespoon lemon juice |
| $1/4$ | cup granulated sugar |

Preheat oven to 350°. Grease a 5" x 9" loaf pan, and set aside. In an electric mixer, cream the shortening, sugar, and eggs until light and fluffy. Measure flour, and sift; then re-measure flour by spooning lightly into a cup. Re-sift flour with baking powder and salt. Beat the dry ingredients into the creamed mixture, alternating with the milk. Stir pecans in by hand. Pour batter into the loaf pan, and bake in the preheated oven for 45-55 minutes or until loaf tests done. If loaf appears to brown too fast, place a loose sheet of aluminum foil on top of the loaf. Remove loaf from the oven, and pierce the entire surface of the loaf with a cocktail pick. Combine the ingredients of the glaze in a small saucepan, and heat to dissolve the sugar. Spoon the hot glaze over the hot loaf of bread. Allow to cool for 45 minutes; then turn out of pan, and dust the top with powdered sugar.

*Light and very delicate. This sweet bread can be frozen and sliced one slice at a time to serve with coffee or tea. It is also perfect as a dessert cake.*

# Peachtop Pastry

*Allow peaches to come to room temperature, if cold.*

| | |
|---|---|
| 1 | egg, separated and room temperature |
| 8 | ounces cream cheese, softened |
| 1 | cup powdered sugar |
| 2 | (8-ounce) cans Pillsbury refrigerated crescent rolls |
| 1 | quart thinly sliced peaches, lightly sweetened with sugar |

Preheat oven to 350°. Spray-grease a cookie pan. In an electric mixer, beat the egg white until very stiff. In another bowl, cream together the cream cheese and sugar. Add the stiff egg white to cream cheese mixture. Unroll 1 can crescent rolls on the cookie pan, and fill the center with ¹/₂ of the cream cheese mixture. Fold the long sides to the middle, then press to seal the ends. Repeat with the other can of rolls. Beat the egg yolk until frothy, and brush on the tops of the pastries. Dust pastry tops with powdered sugar using a sifter. Bake in the preheated oven for 20 minutes. Allow to cool for 5-10 minutes, then slice and top with peach slices. Serves: 12.

# Sour Cream Pancakes with Peach Syrup

Pancakes:

| | | | |
|---|---|---|---|
| $2^1/_2$ | cups plain flour | 3 | eggs |
| 1 | tablespoon baking powder | 2 | cups buttermilk |
| 1 | tablespoon granulated sugar | 1 | cup sour cream |
| 2 | teaspoons soda | 2 | tablespoons margarine, melted |
| 1 | teaspoon salt | | |

In a bowl, sift all dry ingredients together. In another bowl, beat eggs; then add buttermilk and sour cream until blended. Stir in the melted margarine. Cook on a medium hot, greased griddle or skillet until browned and firm. Serves: 8 or more. Top hot pancakes with hot peach syrup (recipe follows).

# Peach Sy

For pancakes, waffles, ice cream . . .

| | |
|---|---|
| 4 | cups fresh peaches, mashed |
| 1 | cup plus 2 tablespoons water, divided |
| 2 | tablespoons lemon juice |
| 1/4 | cup granulated sugar |
| 2 | tablespoons cornstarch |

In a saucepan, combine peaches, 1 cup of the water, lemon juice, and sugar. Heat to boiling, then reduce to simmer for 30 minutes, stirring often. Mix cornstarch with the cold water until smooth; quickly stir into the peach mixture. Cook syrup an additional 5 minutes, stirring constantly. Serve hot over pancakes, waffles, or ice cream. Syrup can be bottled and refrigerated to be served cold over ice cream or heated in the micowave to serve hot again.

# Petite Rolls with Peach Butter

1   cup self-rising flour
3   level tablespoons commercial
    mayonnaise

$^1/_2$   cup milk

Preheat oven to 400°. Combine self-rising flour and mayonnaise. Gradually stir in the milk until just blended. Place the batter into greased mini-muffin pans. Bake in a preheated 400° oven for 12 to 15 minutes or until very light brown.

## Peach Butter

1    cup butter or margarine, softened
$^3/_4$   cup peaches; washed, peeled, and sliced

3    tablespoons powdered sugar
2    ounces cream cheese (optional)

In a blender or food processor, puree the peach slices, sugar, and butter until smooth. Store in a sealed container in the refrigerator.

*To add another delightful flavor to this butter, blend in 2-ounces of softened cream cheese and a little extra sugar.*

# Muffleti

*(oatmeal and fruit muffins)*

| | | | |
|---|---|---|---|
| 4 to 5 | medium peaches, divided | 1 | teaspoon cinnamon |
| 1 | cup plain flour plus 1 tablespoon | 1 | egg |
| 1 | cup old fashioned rolled oats | ¹/₄ | cup vegetable oil |
| ³/₄ | cup brown sugar, packed | ¹/₄ | cup buttermilk |
| 2 | teaspoons baking powder | ¹/₂ | cup raisins |
| | | ¹/₂ | cup pecans, chopped |

Preheat oven to 400°. Line 12 muffin cups with paper cupcake liners or grease the muffin cups. Wash and peel all the peaches; then dice 1 peach, and drain. Puree the remaining peaches to make ³/₄ cup of peach puree. In a large bowl, combine the 1 cup of flour, oats, brown sugar, baking powder, and cinnamon; mix well. In another bowl, beat the egg; then add oil, peach puree, and buttermilk. Pour the liquid ingredients into the flour mixture, and mix until just moistened. In a small bowl, mix the drained, diced peach with the raisins, pecans, and remaining 1 tablespoon flour. Fold the raisin mixture into the batter; mix well. Spoon into the muffin cups, and bake in the preheated oven for 20 minutes or until tested done. Yield: 12 muffins.

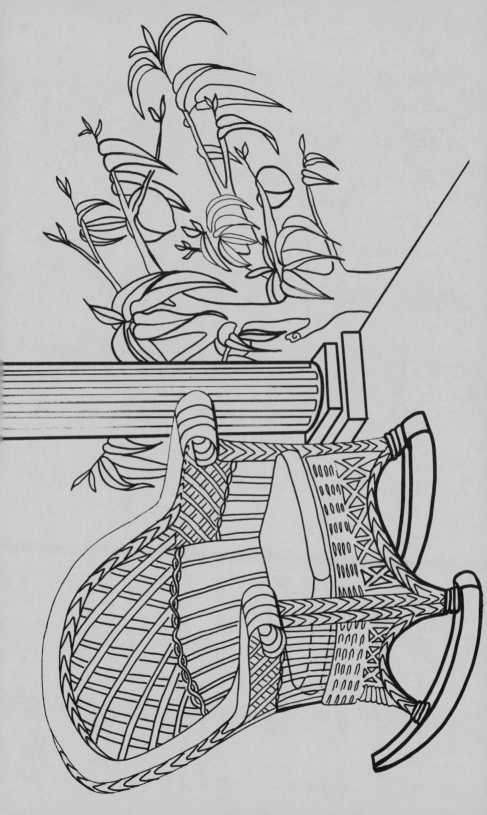

# Desserts

## Paradise Peach Cake

*The recipe requires the cake to be refrigerated for 3 days before serving. Around our house it never even makes it to the refrigerator sometimes!*

1    Duncan Hines Butter Recipe
       Golden Cake Mix

Filling and Icing:

| | |
|---|---|
| 14 | ounces sour cream |
| 3/4 | cup granulated sugar |
| 10 | ounces frozen coconut, thawed |
| 4 | ounces whipped topping, thawed |
| 2 | large peaches; washed, peeled, and mashed |

Lemon juice
Extra granulated sugar
2    fresh peaches; washed and
       peeled for garnish

Make cake as directed on the box for layer cakes. Cool cakes; then slice horizontally. Make filling by mixing sour cream, sugar, and coconut. Reserve 1/2 cup filling to use on top icing. Spoon filling in a layer between each cake layer, and coat sides of cake. For the top of the cake, mix whipped topping with the reserved 1/2 cup filling. Lightly sprinkle the 2 mashed peaches with a few drops lemon juice, and add to the topping mixture; then ice the cake top. Just before serving, cut the remaining 2 peaches into wedges, and toss with a few drops of lemon juice and sugar to taste. Garnish the top of the cake with the peach wedges.

# Peach Torte

| | | |
|---|---|---|
| 1 | package yellow cake mix with pudding | |
| 4 | cups thinly sliced fresh peaches | |
| 14-ounces peach glaze or junior peaches (baby food) | | |
| 6 | ounces cream cheese | |
| $\frac{1}{4}$ | cup granulated sugar | |
| 6 | ounces whipped topping, thawed | |
| $\frac{1}{2}$ | cup powdered sugar | |
| 1 | whole orange; washed, sliced in rings, and cut in half | |

Bake cake according to package instructions for 2 layer cakes; cool completely. Slice the layers in half, and place in the freezer, or freeze the layers then slice frozen. Mix the peach slices with the peach glaze. Reserve 3 tablespoons of the mixture for the top of the cake. In an electric mixer, beat cream cheese, granulated sugar, whipped topping, and powdered sugar until well-blended. On serving platter or cake stand, place a halved layer of the frozen cake. Spread a thin coating of the cream cheese mixture on the layer; then cover with $\frac{1}{3}$ of the glaze mixture. Repeat process with 2 more frozen halved layers. Place the remaining frozen halved layer on top, and cover top of the cake with the cream cheese mixture. Place the reserved 3 tablespoons of glaze mixture in the center of the cake, and decorate with the orange slice halves. Be creative using the orange slices and extra whipped topping. Refrigerate the cake until serving time.

*To transport this cake, allow the cake to be refrigerated until completely cold. Place three wooden bamboo skewers in different locations through all four layers of the cake. Cover the cake with plastic wrap.*

# Glory B Cake *by Brenda*

*This cake can be made quickly by hand without getting out the mixer.*

1    cup  granulated sugar
2    cups  self-rising flour
3    eggs

1    cup  vegetable oil
1    (6-ounce) jar junior peaches (baby food)
1    cup  pecans, chopped

Preheat oven to 350°. Grease a Bundt or tube pan, and set aside. In another bowl, beat the eggs lightly; then beat in the oil and the peaches. Add the egg mixture to the flour mixture, and beat by hand for 1-2 minutes. Fold in chopped pecans. Pour into the greased pan. Bake in the preheated oven for 35-40 minutes.

# Fresh Peach Cobbler

| | | |
|---|---|---|
| 1 | package Pillsbury All-Ready pie crust | |
| 1 | quart sliced fresh peeled peaches | |
| 3/4 | cup water | |
| 3/4 | | cup granulated sugar |
| 1/4 | | cup margarine, cut in slices |

Preheat oven to 425°. Unfold one pie crust, and slice into strips. Place unfolded remaining pie crust into a deep round baking dish. Make a layer of 1/2 the peach slices, then add the water. Sprinkle evenly with 1/2 the sugar, and dot with 1/2 the margarine slices. Place 1/2 the pastry strips in a lattice design on top. Repeat with a layer of peach slices, sugar, margarine, and finish with remaining pastry strips in the lattice design. Place on a preheated cookie sheet. Cook in a preheated oven at 425° until mixture bubbles; then reduce heat to 250°, and bake for 30 to 45 minutes depending on thickness and ripeness of peaches.

*Best and easiest cobbler that I have ever made. Not too sweet, very light, and crisp.*

# French Crumb Pie

| | |
|---|---|
| 5 | large fresh peaches |
| 1 | cup brown sugar |
| 2 | tablespoons plain flour |
| 1/4 | teaspoon cinnamon |
| 1 | tablespoon lemon juice |
| 1 | unbaked deep-dish 9-inch pie shell |

Topping:

| | |
|---|---|
| 3/4 | cup brown sugar |
| 1/4 | teaspoon nutmeg |
| 1 | cup plain flour |
| 1/2 | cup margarine, melted |

Preheat oven to 350°. Wash, peel, and slice peaches. Mix together brown sugar, flour, and cinnamon. Pour lemon juice over peaches; then stir together the peaches and the sugar mixture. Place in unbaked pie shell. Mix together all topping ingredients until well-blended; then crumble evenly over top of the peaches in the pie shell. Bake in the preheated oven for 45 minutes.

*Not too sweet, not too tart——juuust right!*

# Peach Pie A La Mode

| | |
|---|---|
| 5 | medium fresh peaches |
| 1 | tablespoon lemon juice |
| 1 | unbaked 9-inch pie shell |
| 3/4 | cup granulated sugar |

| | |
|---|---|
| 2 | eggs, beaten |
| 2 | tablespoons melted margarine |
| 1/2 | cup pecans, chopped coarsely |
| | Vanilla ice cream |

Preheat oven to 425°. Wash, peel, and slice peaches; drain. In a bowl, toss the peaches with the lemon juice; then place peach slices into the pie shell. Mix together the sugar, eggs, melted margarine, and pecans. Pour the egg mixture over the peaches. Bake in the preheated oven for 25-30 minutes. Serve with ice cream on top. Serves 6-8.

# Peach Cloud Pie

*Make at least 2 hours before serving. The crust can be made one day in advance, cooled completely, and wrapped tightly in plastic wrap and foil.*

| | |
|---|---|
| 3 | egg whites, at room temperature |
| ³/₄ | cup granulated sugar |
| 16 | soda crackers, crushed |
| ¹/₄ | teaspoon baking powder |
| ¹/₂ | cup pecans, chopped |
| 6 | large fresh peaches |
| | Extra sugar |
| ¹/₂ | pint whipping cream |

Preheat oven to 325°. In an electric mixer, beat egg whites until very stiff; then fold the sugar in by hand. Mix the crushed crackers, baking powder, and pecans; gently fold these into the egg white mixture. Pour the egg mixture into a greased round or square 8-inch baking dish making a slight indentation in the center like a pie crust. Bake in the preheated oven for 30 minutes, then allow the crust to completely cool. Wash, peel, and slice peaches in wedges, and sweeten to taste. Just before serving, arrange the peach wedges on the cooled crust. Whip the cream, and sweeten to taste. Add the whipped cream to the top of the peaches in dollops allowing the peaches to be seen.

*Crisp and light as a cloud!*

Desserts

# Peach Island Creme Pie

| | |
|---|---|
| 1 | envelope unflavored gelatin |
| 1/4 | cup cold water |
| 1 | cup mashed peaches |
| 1/2 | cup Coco Lopez cream of coconut |
| 1/4 | cup rum |

| | |
|---|---|
| 1/2 | pint whipping cream, whipped and divided |
| 1 | 8-inch graham cracker crumb pie shell |
| 1 | large fresh peach; washed, peeled, and sliced in wedges |
| | Lemon juice |
| | Sugar |

Soften gelatin in cold water. Heat the mashed peaches in a 10-inch skillet to boiling; then stir in gelatin mixture until completely dissolved. Add Coco Lopez and rum. Chill in refrigerator or freezer until almost set (don't forget it!) Fold in 1/2 of the whipped cream, and pour into the pie shell. Refrigerate until firm; then spread the remaining whipped cream, sweetened to taste, evenly on top. Sprinkle a little lemon juice on the peach wedges to help them keep their color; then lightly sprinkle with sugar to taste. Arrange the peach wedges in a design to give the finishing touch.

*Wow! The hint of rum and the taste of the islands all blended with the softness of the South!*

# Magic Cobbler

| | |
|---|---|
| 1/2 | cup margarine |
| 1 | cup plain flour |
| 1 | cup granulated sugar, divided |
| 1/2 | teaspoon salt |
| 3 | teaspoons baking powder |

| | |
|---|---|
| 1 | cup milk |
| 3 | full cups sliced fresh peaches |
| 1/4 | teaspoon cinnamon |
| | Vanilla ice cream (optional) |

Preheat oven to 350°. Melt the margarine in a 9" x 13" baking dish, then coat bottom and sides of dish with the melted margarine. In a food processor or blender, mix flour, 1/2 cup of the sugar, salt, baking powder, and milk until well blended. Evenly spread peach slices over the bottom of the baking dish; then pour the milk mixture over peaches. Sprinkle with the remaining 1/2 cup sugar mixed with the cinnamon. Bake in the preheated oven for 35 minutes. The crust will magically appear to cover the entire surface. Allow cobbler to cool for 5 minutes, then serve topped with ice cream, if desired.

*This recipe can be doubled using a larger baking dish or two 9" x 13" baking dishes. Just double all the ingredients.*

# Desserts

# Peach Fluff

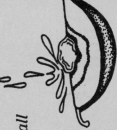

| | | | |
|---|---|---|---|
| 1 | cup fresh sliced peaches | 1 | tablespoon lemon juice |
| 1/4 | cup granulated sugar | 1 1/4 | cup whipped topping, thawed |
| 1 | egg yolk | | |

Place all ingredients except whipped topping into a blender or food processor with steel blade; puree. Gently fold in the whipped topping by hand. Pour into compotes or other suitable bowls and chill in the refrigerator. Serves: 2.

*Very light dessert to add the final delicious touch. To make a grand variation, add a small amount of brandy.*

# Really Peachy Cheesecake Squares

| | |
|---|---|
| 1/3 | cup margarine, cut into chunks |
| 1/3 | cup firmly packed brown sugar |
| 1 | cup plain flour |
| 1/4 | cup granulated sugar |
| 8 | ounces cream cheese, softened |

| | |
|---|---|
| 1 | egg |
| 1 | tablespoon lemon juice |
| 1 | cup diced fresh peaches |
| 1/2 | cup pecans, chopped |

Preheat oven to 350°. In food processor using the steel blade, place the margarine, brown sugar, and flour; blend into crumbs. Reserve 1/2 cup of this mixture for topping. Press remaining mixture into an 8-inch square greased baking dish. Bake at 350° for 10-12 minutes. In an electric mixer, cream the granulated sugar and cream cheese; then add egg and lemon juice. Beat on medium speed for 1-2 minutes; stir in diced peaches and the pecans. Spread the peach mixture over the crust, and sprinkle top with remaining crumb mixture. Bake at 350° for 25 minutes or until filling is set and the top is lightly browned. Cool and cut into squares. Refrigerate to store. Cut into small squares–these are rich.

*How can you miss on this one? Cheesecake with a crisp cookie crunch on the bottom and peaches and pecans on the top!*

# Carolina Crunch

7       large firm ripe peaches
$\frac{1}{2}$   cup margarine
$\frac{3}{4}$   cup granulated sugar

1       cup plain flour
        Vanilla ice cream (optional)

Wash, peel, and cut peaches into thick wedges; drain. Place the wedges into a greased 2-quart baking dish. Melt the margarine; then stir in the sugar, and mix well. Add flour and mix again. Spread the thick mixture over the top of the peaches as evenly as possible. Some small areas may not be totally covered. Bake at 350° for 45-55 minutes or until peaches are cooked and the top is light brown. Allow to cool for 10 minutes. Serve topped with ice cream, if desired. Serves: 4-6.

# Cookie Peach Shortcake

*A no-cook dessert*

| | |
|---|---|
| 2 | cups sliced fresh peaches |
| | Sugar to taste |
| ¹/₂ | pint whipping cream (aerosol whipped cream or whipped topping can be used) |
| 1 | (10-ounce) package Lorna Doone cookies |

Place the sliced peaches into a bowl, and add sugar to taste. Cover and refrigerate. Whip cream in cold bowl with cold electric mixer beaters; add sugar to taste. On individual dessert plates, place 4 cookies on each plate. Add 1 to 2 tablespoons sliced peaches, and top with whipped cream; repeat the layers. Serve immediately to keep the cookies crisp. Serves: 4.

*My mother served this easy dessert when I was a child, and it remains a favorite.*

# Desserts

# Alice's Spiked Peaches

1 to 2 large fresh peaches per person
Lemon juice
Sugar

A choice of: Grenadine syrup
Creme de menthe, liqueur or syrup
Brandy

Use large unblemished fresh peaches peeled by dropping the whole unpeeled peach into boiling water for a few minutes, then plunging into cold water. The skin of the peach comes off in large pieces of peel. Cut into large, pretty wedges. Sprinkle with a few drops of lemon juice. Lightly sweeten the peaches with sugar. Place wedges in a short, wide glass and add 2 tablespoons of grenadine syrup, creme de menthe liqueur or syrup, or brandy per peach. Refrigerate the peaches at least 24 hours. Serve over vanilla ice cream topped with whipped cream or whipped topping.

*Thanks, Alice, the peaches are beautiful. The red and green peaches are particularly pretty at Christmas time!*

# Fresh Fruit Dip

9    ounces whipped topping, thawed
4    ounces sour cream

$^1/_4$ to $^1/_2$ cup of a sweet liqueur (peach, Amaretto, Grand Marnier, etc.)

1    (3-ounce) package instant vanilla pudding

In a bowl, blend the whipped topping, sour cream, and liqueur; then sprinkle with the dry pudding mix. Mix well, cover, and refrigerate until cold. This is a dipping sauce for fresh fruit. Use peach wedges, strawberries, pineapple, apple, cantaloupe, grapes, etc.

# Vanilla Peach Ice Cream

| | | |
|---|---|---|
| 1 | | quart milk |
| 4 | | eggs |
| $1^3/_4$ | | cups granulated sugar, divided 3 ways |
| | $^1/_2$ | pint whipping cream |
| | 3 | cups mashed peaches |

Rinse a $1^1/_2$ quart saucepan in cold water; do not dry. Add the milk to the saucepan and cook over medium heat until a film forms on top of the milk. Test frequently with a fork, by dipping the fork into the milk and slowly pulling the fork back up. If a film comes up with the fork, then the milk is scalded. Scalding will occur before the milk boils. Set the scaled milk aside to cool. Beat the eggs with $^1/_2$ cup of the sugar; then slowly add the cooled scalded milk to the eggs while stirring constantly. Pour this mixture into the top of a double boiler, cover, and cook over boiling water for 20 minutes; do not stir during this cooking. Add $^3/_4$ cup sugar to the peaches and mix well. After the custard has cooked; remove from heat and allow to cool. Whip the cream in a chilled bowl, and add $^1/_2$ cup of the sugar when cream is stiff. When the egg custard has cooled, fold in the whipped cream and the peaches; freeze in an electric ice cream freezer or give it a good cranking in an old fashioned hand crank freezer.

*Remember the olden days of front porches, large comfortable rocking chairs, and paper fans on wooden handles — does it seem to you that a lot of the advertisements on the fans were for funeral homes?*

# Red, White, and Peach Parfait

## Desserts

*Make the parfaits at least one day in advance of serving*

| | |
|---|---|
| 8 | ounces frozen raspberries, thawed |
| 1/2 | cup currant or red plum jelly |
| 1 1/2 | teaspoons cornstarch |
| 1 | tablespoon cold water |

| | |
|---|---|
| 1 | quart vanilla ice cream |
| | Thinly sliced fresh peaches, sweetened lightly |
| | Sweetened whipped cream or whipped topping |

In a saucepan, blend the raspberries and jelly; and cook while mashing the berries until boiling. Remove from heat. In a small bowl, mix the cornstarch with the cold water, and stir into the raspberry mixture. Simmer until the mixture is thickened and clear. Strain into a bowl to remove seeds, and allow sauce to cool. Using parfait glasses, make layers: sauce, peaches, ice cream, peaches, sauce, ice cream, peaches, sauce. Freeze the parfaits. When ready to serve, allow 15 to 20 minutes of thawing time before serving. Top with a dollop of whipped cream and 3 drops of sauce. Makes eight 8-ounce parfaits.

*A tart, tangy flavor to match the dazzling colors of the layers.*

# Pralined Peach Ice Cream

| | |
|---|---|
| 5 | tablespoons margarine |
| 1 | cup brown sugar, packed |
| $^1/_2$ | cup Half and Half |
| 1 | cup pecans, chopped |

Lorna Doone cookies
Fresh peach slices
Vanilla ice cream

In a saucepan, melt margarine, and add brown sugar. Cook over low heat, stirring constantly, for about 5 to 7 minutes. Remove from heat, and gradually stir in the Half and Half. Return to heat, and cook for 1 minute. Fold in the pecans, and stir. On individual dessert plates, place 4 cookies on each plate. Add 1 or 2 tablespoons of the peaches, top with a scoop of ice cream. Drizzle the hot praline sauce over the ice cream. If any sauce is left, it can be cooled and refrigerated to be heated at a later time. Yield: $1^1/_2$ cups.

*If you long for the flavors of the Deep South — This is it! So simple to be so good. Surely when you're eatin' this you can see the riverboat comin' 'round 'th bend.*

# Fresh Peach Sherbet

| | | |
|---|---|---|
| 4 | | eggs, separated |
| 4 | | cups fresh peaches; washed, peeled, and diced very fine (about 5 large peaches) |
| | 1 | cup powdered sugar, sifted |
| | 1 | (14-ounce) can sweetened condensed milk |
| | $1/4$ | cup reconstituted lemon juice |

Separate eggs, and let them come to room temperature. Combine peaches and sugar; toss carefully to coat. In a large bowl, combine milk, lemon juice, and egg yolks; blend well. Stir in peaches. Beat the room temperature egg whites until stiff, but not dry. Fold into peach mixture, and pour into a 9" x 13" dish. Cover with foil, and freeze for about $1^1/_2$ to 2 hours or until a firm mush forms. Turn the mixture into a large, chilled bowl, and break into pieces. Beat until fluffy, but not melted. Quickly return to the dish, and freeze. Allow to freeze for about 2 hours or until very firm. Yield: $1/_2$ gallon.

# Index

**GENE WESTBROOK PUBLICTIONS,** P.O. Box 869 Millbrook, AL 36054 OR TOLL FREE ORDER 1-800-536-5407

Please send me _____ copies of POSITIVELY PEACHY, (Includes Postage & Handling) @ $7.65 each _____

(Or 3 for $17.85 plus $4.25 postage)

Alabama Residents add 4% sales tax _____

Gift Wrap _____ @ .24 each _____

@ 1.00 each _____

Total Enclosed _____

Print Name _____

Address _____

City _____ State _____ Zip _____

Checks to: Gene Westbrook Publications, Inc. or Charge to:

Visa _____ MC _____ Acc.# _____

Print Name _____

Exp. Date _____ Signature _____

- - - - - - - - - - - - - - - - - - - - - - - - - - - - - - - - - - - - - - - - - - - - - - -

**GENE WESTBROOK PUBLICTIONS,** P.O. Box 869 Millbrook, AL 36054 OR TOLL FREE ORDER 1-800-536-5407

Please send me _____ copies of POSITIVELY PEACHY, (Includes Postage & Handling) @ $7.65 each _____

(Or 3 for $17.85 plus $4.25 postage)

Alabama Residents add 4% sales tax _____

Gift Wrap _____ @ .24 each _____

@ 1.00 each _____

Total Enclosed _____

Print Name _____

Address _____

City _____ State _____ Zip _____

Checks to: Gene Westbrook Publications, Inc. or Charge to:

Visa _____ MC _____ Acc.# _____

Print Name _____

Exp. Date _____ Signature _____